WOLF IN THE RIVER

Adam Rapp

BROADWAY PLAY PUBLISHING INC
224 E 62nd St, NY, NY 10065
www.broadwayplaypub.com
info@broadwayplaypub.com

WOLF IN THE RIVER
© Copyright 2017 Adam Rapp

Cover art by Brad Mead

First edition: September 2017
I S B N: 978-0-88145-723-0

Book design: Marie Donovan
Page make-up: Adobe InDesign
Typeface: Palatino

WOLF IN THE RIVER was commissioned and originally produced in the fall of 2015 by the National Institute of Dramatic Art in Sydney, Australia. It was directed by the author with the following cast and creative contribuors:

THE WOLF	Jack Ellis
TANA WEED	Georgia Wilkinson-Derums
MONTY MAE MALONEY	Xanthe Paige
ANSEL "PIN" PINWOOD	Thomas Pidd
AIKIN	Thuso Lepwake
DOTHAN WEED	Brenden Dodds
DEBO	Charles Wu

Director	Adam Rapp
Sets	Charlotte Henery
Costumes	Michael Hili
Sound	Gayda de Mesa
Lights	Kristy Walker
Production stage manager	Fraser Orford

WOLF IN THE RIVER was produced Off-Broadway at The Flea Theatre in the spring of 2016 with the following cast and creative contributors:

THE WOLF	Jack Ellis/Olivia Jampol
TANA WEED	Kate Thulin
MONTY MAE MALONEY	Xanthe Paige/ Kristin Friedlander
ANSEL "PIN" PINWOOD	Mike Swift
AIKIN	Karen Eilbacher
DOTHAN WEED	William Apps
DEBO	Maki Borden
THE LOST CHOIR	Alexandra Curran, Jack Horton Gilbert, John Paul Harkins, Artem Kreimer, Derek Christopher Murphy Casey Wortmann

Director	Adam Rapp
Sets	Arnulfo Maldonado
Costumes	Michael Hili & Hallie Elizabeth Newton
Sound	Brendan Connelly
Lights	Masha Tsimring
Fight choreographer	J David Brimmer
Assistant director	Anne Cecelia Haney
Production stage manager	Morgan Leigh Beach

CHARACTERS

THE WOLF, *a man, a wolf, a shapechanger.*

TANA WEED, *caucasian. A girl, 16, ready.*

DEBO, *a boy from Benton, Illinois. Loves* TANA.

DOTHAN WEED, TANA's *older brother, a dishonorably discharged, displaced veteran, twenties, lost feeling, a toy thief, says very little.*

MONTY MAE MALONEY, *caucasian.* DOTHAN's *girlfriend, twenties, the kingpin, a blood collector.*

AIKIN, *African-American.* MONTY's *lieutenant, twenties, eats flowers, an addict.*

ANSEL PINWOOD (PIN), *caucasian.* MONTY's *lesser footsoldier, twenties, a dreamer, harbors feelings for* TANA.

DUMPTRUCK LORNA, *played by* THE MAN, MONTY's *mother, lives in the basement, always in a La-Z-Boy, watches* Judge Judy, *superstitious.*

THE LOST CHOIR, *a collection of six lost souls—four male, two female—who haunt the play in various ways. They are ghosts who have perished in the river.*

SETTING

A bare, impoverished space. A mound of dark earth, spindly purplish flowers sprouting here and there. The audience encircles the playing space in many orphaned chairs. Included in this arrangement is an old La-Z-Boy, a standing lamp beside it. Also in the circle of chairs, a refrigerator.

Outside the perimeter of the chairs, in other heaps of earth, are mason jars, jugs, and other glass receptacles, which are filled with blood and sealed with cork, aluminum foil, cloth and shoelaces, etc.

(The sound of a refrigerator hum. This hum is alive when the audience enters the space.)

(After the audience is seated and the theater doors are closed, a man from the audience rises from one of the chairs, removes his shirt. This is the WOLF. He removes his shoes, sets them down quietly. He then snaps, and the lights bump brighter. He begins counting each audience member, now shouldering a nondescript canvas sack. He moves about the space as he wishes.)

WOLF: One, two, three, four, five, six, seven, eight, nine, ten, eleven, twelve, thirteen, fourteen, fifteen, sixteen, seventeen, eighteen, nineteen, twenty, twenty-one, twenty-two, twenty-three, twenty-four, twenty-five, twenty-six, twenty-seven, twenty-eight, twenty-nine, thirty, thirty-one, thirty-two, thirty-three, thirty-four, thirty-five, thirty-six, thirty-seven, thirty-eight, thirty-nine, forty, forty-one, forty-two, forty-three, forty-four, forty-five, forty-six, forty-seven, forty-eight, forty-nine, fifty, fifty-one, fifty-two, fifty-three, fifty-four, fifty-five, fifty-six, fifty-seven, fifty-eight, fifty-nine, *(Points to himself)* sixty. *(Speaking directly to the audience now)* You're prolly wonderin' who I am, right? Who is that unremarkable figure in loose pants, enumerating us like heads of cabbage? Like things you keep in a bin? Why'd he just walk up there like that? Only moments ago he was sittin' right over there. *(He gestures to the person he was sitting beside).* He was sittin' next to me, dangit, and now he's up there talkin', bumpin' at the gums about this and that, showin' off. He certainly looks regular. Smells regular. He's got regular eyes.

Regular parts. He sounds average enough. *(From the canvas sack, he produces a muddy dress.)*

WOLF: Little sundress with bluebells on it. Pretty ain't it?

(He drops the dress, produces muddy panties.)

WOLF: Panties.

(He sniffs them, drops the panties, produces muddy cutoff jean shorts.)

WOLF: Jean shorts.

(He drops the shorts, produces a pair of muddy black Sketcher sneakers.)

WOLF: She prolly got these at the Payless. Size seven.

(He drops the Sketchers, produces a cell phone.)

WOLF: And one of these, of course. The Fall of Man.

(He drops the cell phone. All of the items from the bag are now in a heap at his feet.)

WOLF: I'm the one who ate her... No, I ain't. *(He points to someone in the audience)* He did it! *(He points to a woman)* Or maybe it was her. *(Points to another)* Or this citizen here, inconspicuous as a post in the ground... Are you a citizen? What are you, anyway?

(He points to a spot.)

WOLF: It happened right over there, in the mud. Sweat bees. Coupla crushed Miller Hi-Lifes. Condoms. Good fishin' spot actually. That's where they found four of her teeth anyway... Oh, she was full of the river, yeah she was full up.
I might be lyin', of course. I'm prolly not... But I might be. The truth and the lie are tricky little fish ain't they? Tricky as trout during a thunderstorm.
In case y'all haven't noticed, I'm a wolf. See this smile? These claws? The fun in my eyes? Can you smell me?

I can smell you, and you, and you, and you, and you, and you. You smell like horses. And you smell like a fire. I can smell the parts you try to hide. The places where you keep fear and pleasure and glumness. Are you glum, friend? Are you a glum little chicken? Would you like to walk with me a while?

So if I'm a wolf, who are you? I know you been thinkin' about that? *If he's a wolf then who am I?* Y'all are the river. Yes, that's what you are. An angry, undulatin', rip-roarin' river. You go for miles and your current's so strong this time a year that the people in this town string ropes across to help folks get to the other side. Oh, sometimes I'm the river, too. And sometimes you're the wolf. That's the fun part of the riddle. That's how come I left a part of me out there with you. Just so y'all can be reminded of that.

Go at the neck first. This way they stop screamin'. All you can hear is the trees breathin'. The way they murmur. Trees keepin' secrets. The burbling of the body's water. The gentler sounds.

Humans are born with three hundred bones. By the time a person reaches adulthood that number goes down to about two-hundred and six. Nobody really knows why. Where do all those bones go?

I think that girl had about two-twelve, maybe two-thirteen. That's what I heard, at least. She was losin' bones.

I like the face. The eyeballs. The hands. The stomach. The liver. The saucy humors. The heart ain't no bigger'n a fist…

(The theater doors burst open and a girl rushes into the space. She stops at the threshold of the mound of earth. She is lost, naked, has been running for her life. She unsure of where she is. She looks up at the WOLF, *turns around, but another figure, a ghostly member of the* LOST CHOIR, *blocks her escape.)*

(A loud heartbeat can be heard, slow and awful.)

(She approaches the man. He circles her once, smells her thoroughly, crotch-to-neck, moves away from her. The heartbeat quickens. The WOLF *beats his chest to the quickening heartbeat. Others from the darkness, members of the* LOST CHOIR, *join in. Yelps can be heard in the darkness, savage and delirious. Encroaching figures can be seen here and there.)*

(The girl gathers the sundress, the Sketchers, the panties, and cell phone into her arms.)

(Terrified, she turns toward the yelps, and approaching figures.)

(Blackout. Night)

(Crickets. Treefrogs. Cicadas. An owl)

(A refrigerator door is opened, the only source of light. TANA, *the girl we had just encountered, stands before it, barefoot, wearing only a thin cotton dress that might be a nightgown, the cold air cooling her back. She is sixteen, talking on her cell phone.)*

(On top of the refrigerator, a portable C D player.)

(Somewhere the figure of a boy, DEBO, *is illuminated. He is nowhere and everywhere, in her head, in her phone, in every passing shadow. They are in love.)*

DEBO: You still there?

TANA: Yes.

DEBO: You can hear me okay?

TANA: I can hear you perfect.

DEBO: What's that humming?

TANA: My fridge.

DEBO: You makin' somethin'?

TANA: Just standin' in front of it.

DEBO: It's hot, huh?

TANA: It's dumbdumb hot. The air's like medicine on you.

DEBO: You're dumbdumb hot.

TANA: …You stop carin' about the mosquitoes. You just let 'em have at you.

DEBO: It was ninety-three today. And humid. The trees were sweatin'.

TANA: You got mosquitoes there?

DEBO: Size of Toyotas.

TANA: I like when you talk cars.

DEBO: You're a car.

TANA: Oh yeah, what kinda car am I?

DEBO: A G. T. O.

TANA: I don't even know what that means.

DEBO: Prettiest engine you'll ever see.

TANA: You're a car.

DEBO: I know I'm a car.

TANA: What kind?

DEBO: I'm a Sixty-Nine Dodge Dart. Dragged out with a vented hood.

TANA: What color?

DEBO: Black as night.

TANA: Debo Debo Debo.

DEBO: Tana Tana Tana.

TANA: I can be mean.

DEBO: I doubt it…

TANA: I don't got no manners. I chew with my mouth open. And I burp like a goat.

DEBO: We got goats. A lot of 'em got faces like dead men on money.

TANA: You got cows, too, ain't it?

DEBO: Fifty head of black angus. Dark as obsidian. Meadows so long and green they look like they're floatin' on water.

TANA: What's obsidian?

DEBO: Volcanic rock.

TANA: They got volcanoes up in Illinois?

DEBO: No, but I read about 'em. And it's Illinois (*Silent "s"*).

(DEBO *and* TANA *are both swooning.*)

DEBO: Everything's just dumb till I talk to you.

TANA: *(Pleased)* It's just awful, ain't it?

DEBO: I can't wait to see you.

TANA: Me too.

DEBO: That picture you sent's been drivin' me crazy.

TANA: Which one?

DEBO: The one where you're wearin' those red sunglasses. Man.

(*From the refrigerator's butter cubby* TANA *produces a pair of red sunglasses, puts them on.*)

DEBO: When I look at that picture I can feel your heart beatin'.

TANA: Where?

DEBO: In my mouth. I can taste it.

TANA: What's it taste like?

DEBO: I don't know. You.

TANA: Tell me about the willow tree again?

(TANA *begins walking the circle between the audience and the mound of earth. With only a flashlight illuminating his path,* DEBO *walks outside the perimeter of the chairs, in the opposite direction. He is mostly in shadow, save for the faint bit of illumination produced by his cellphone.*)

DEBO: It's in my back yard. Biggest willow you're likely to see. Sometimes people knock on the front door and ask if they can take pictures of it. Complete strangers drive from miles away. Come all the way from Chicago. When you lie under it the world goes away.

TANA: Where does it go?

DEBO: Wherever you want it to.

TANA: What are them branches called again?

DEBO: Catkins.

TANA: *(Loving the word)* Catkins.

DEBO: They're a-petalous flowers.

TANA: A-petalous. Sounds like a song.

DEBO: You're a song.

TANA: I can't even sing.

DEBO: I bet you can.

TANA: I sound like a shot dog.

DEBO: I'm gonna take you out in this pontoon boat. We can lie down on it, stare up at the stars.

TANA: And you'll tickle my arm.

DEBO: Tickle more than that.

TANA: Don't get sassy.

DEBO: You love it.

TANA: …I keep listenin' to your mix. I like that fourth song. The one about the people horses.

DEBO: Purple horses.

TANA: Purple horses. That's pretty.

DEBO: *(Singing)*
Come ride with me on purple horses...

TANA: I hope you still like me.

DEBO: I liked you the minute I laid eyes.

TANA: But that was a while ago.

DEBO: You didn't go and get ugly on me, now, did you?

TANA: No. But what if I smell bad?

DEBO: You smell like peaches.

TANA: How do you know?

DEBO: Cuz I remember. Sweet dirty peaches.

(TANA smells herself.)

TANA: You're just smitten.

DEBO: You're damn right I'm smitten.

(A brief silence)

(MONTY, a young woman, enters from behind the refrigerator, mostly in silhouette. She's been listening. TANA removes her sunglasses, quickly places them back in the butter cubby, retreats toward the dirt.)

DEBO: You still there?

TANA: Uh-huh.

DEBO: I can't wait to finally hold you.

TANA: Me too.

(TANA sits in the dirt. MONTY stands over her.)

DEBO: You're still comin', right?

(No answer)

DEBO: Tana, you there? ...Tana?

(Black out)

(Lights up)

(Bright kitchen light)

(A half-naked male figure can be seen sprinting around the perimeter of chairs with a large inflatable blow-up doll. He lands on the mound's summit, mounts the blow-up doll, thrusts into it. This is PIN. *He is early twenties. He wears an old T-shirt and nothing else . A medical port for taking blood has been crudely Ace bandaged and duct-taped to his upper arm. The blow-up doll's face has somehow been covered with a color-Xerox copy of the face of Miley Cyrus.)*

*(*TANA *is in the dirt. On her feet she wears Sketchers sneakers.)*

*(*AIKIN, *African-American, also shirtless, tattooed, dim teeth. He is arranging the purple flowers that are sprouting out of the dirt in* TANA'*s hair. Like* PIN, *there is a medical port crudely attached to his arm.)*

*(*TANA'*s older brother,* DOTHAN, *shirtless, sits over a collection of gutted, hacked electronic games, with which he is deeply involved in some convoluted, insane-looking process. There is a tattoo on his chest, over his heart, crudely fashioned, Arabic characters. He always wears headphones, large, chunky ones, and most of his things, including his clothes, are riddled with bits of electric tape.)*

(Among the collection of hacked into electronic toys are three small re-purposed analogue tape decks, and an old kick amp. There are many toys scattered all about the mound of earth. DOTHAN'*s attention to this chaos borders on devotional. Like* PIN *and* AIKIN, *an intravenous medical port has been crudely inserted into the meat of his arm.)*

*(*MONTY, *the ruler of this world, stands over* PIN, *at the top of the mound, rallying him on with a wrathful lunacy. Slight and wiry, Monty wears a sports bra, short shorts, no shoes. She commandeers a walking cane with an alligator head, though she walks just fine. She uses the cane for many purposes. She runs shit in this world. Like* TANA, *she does not have a medical port in her arm.)*

MONTY: *(To the blow-up doll)* You like that, Miley?! You arrogant backwater lesbo?! Try twerkin' now, skank! *(To AIKIN)* That pussy's so torn up you couldn't sell it at a bait shop.

(AIKIN giggles.)

MONTY: Turn that donkey-faced skeezer out, Pin. Crack that lesbo pussy!

(PIN continues raping the blow-up doll.)

PIN: GENESIS, EXODUS, LEVITICUS, ASBESTOS, CHICKEN BREASTUS, SNUFFLEUPAGUS, FORD TAURUS, BURRITOS AS BIG AS YOUR HEAD!

(MONTY stabs the blow-up doll with a pocket knife, which hisses and deflates, ending the game.)

(Everything stops, falls silent.)

(MONTY produces a rag from the back of her shorts, drops it on PIN.)

MONTY: Clean the mess off that skank. She dirty.

(PIN cleans the blowup doll.)

MONTY: Bury that skeezer.

(PIN fold the deflated blow-up doll into fours, stuffs it under an audience chair. He finds his track pants, legs into them. He produces a cigarette, sets it between his lips. He eats the cigarette. He produces a heavy chain, begins watching it slowly undulate in his hands.)

(AIKIN continues praying to a cluster of purple flowers.)

(DOTHAN has paid very little attention to any of this and continues tending to his mess of toys.)

(TANA simply sits there, trying to stay alive in this horrible place.)

MONTY: *(To TANA)* Lesson over, lesson leanred. *(Pointing to TANA's Sketchers)* Take those off.

(TANA *removes her shoes.* MONTY *takes them, begins walking slowly around the space, quietly assessing. She sings a verse from Miley Cyrus'* Wrecking Ball.)

(PIN *continues playing with the heavy, rusted chain.* AIKIN *stares at the purple flowers.*)

(DOTHAN *is lost in his world of toys.*)

MONTY: Tana, what's that you're wearin'?

TANA: *(Turned toward the fridge)* A dress.

MONTY: Looks like a fuckin' nightgown to me. Where'd you get it?

TANA: Nowhere.

MONTY: The Nowhere Store? I didn't know the Nowhere Store made nightgowns… You got that piece of shit over at Bobby Homo's, didn't you? Low-rent faggit shoulda been borned female. A growed-assed man obsessed with women's clothes. Knows more about dresses than a slaughterhouse knows slaughterin', aint it Aikin.

(AIKIN *giggles.*)

MONTY: What's that pattern sposed to be?

TANA: Bluebells.

MONTY: They look like fuckin' batwings to me.

TANA: Batwings ain't blue.

MONTY: Neither are bluebells. Batwings on a nightgown? Pin, don't that look like a fuckin' nightgown?

PIN: Yup.

MONTY: Aikin, don't that thing Tana's wearin' look like a garment to be worn in a nocturnal fashion?

(AIKIN *giggles.*)

MONTY: Tana, get me a High Life.

(TANA *crosses to the refrigerator, gets a can of Miller High Life, shuts the door, crosses to* MONTY, *opens it, hands it to her.* MONTY *continues holding her shoes, drinks.* TANA *crosses back to the refrigerator, sits.*)

AIKIN: Can I get one?

MONTY: Only Dothan gets to drink my High Lifes. Ask me why, Pin.

PIN: *(Perfunctory)* Why does Dothan get to drink your High Lifes?

MONTY: Cuz he served our country, ain't it, Dothan? He's a patriot. He did his soldierly duty.

(MONTY *moves to* DOTHAN, *who is in his own world.*)

MONTY: He 's a U-S-of-A, star-spangled veteran. *(To* DOTHAN*)* Your sister's stupid if she thinks she's leavin' the house—

(DOTHAN *rises with a handheld electronic game. The room stops. It's as if a dangerous animal has been awakened. He approaches the refrigerator, opens it, places the toy inside, closes the refrigerator, takes a few steps back. waits, anticipating something extraordinary. After a breath he approaches the refrigerator, opens it. The toy is still just a toy. Disappointed, he removes the toy, returns to where he was, dropping the toy in the dirt. Everyone but* MONTY *deflates to their prior positions, somewhere low and close to the cool earth.*)

(TANA *takes a step toward the discarded toy.*)

MONTY: Sit the fuck down.

(TANA *does so.*)

MONTY: Tell her why she ain't leavin' the house in that, Aikin.

AIKIN: Cause we can see your titties.

MONTY: You must like puttin' them little titties of yours on display.

AIKIN: You can see her cunt too.

MONTY: She must be crazy for it.

AIKIN: Crazy like a cuckoofish.

MONTY: She prolly ain't even got her period yet.

(AIKIN *slurps like a cuckoo fish.*)

MONTY: You get your period yet, Tana? Need Monty Mae to show you how to install a Tampax?

TANA: No.

MONTY: The fuck you don't. Virgin. (*To* DOTHAN) She walks out the door like that she's askin' for it.

PIN: Why can't I get a High Life?

(MONTY *hurls her beer at* PIN.)

MONTY: What's wrong, Pin? You don't like other people talkin' about Tana's tight little pussy?

(PIN *looks down, deferential.*)

MONTY: Newsflash, Dummy: I got a pussy! That gives me the right to talk about pussy all day. Monty Mae Maloney can talk pussy ad nauseum. You know what that means, Pin? Of course you don't. It means endlessly. To a sickening or disgusting degree. Dimwit… Put some panties on, Tana.

TANA: I'm wearin' panties.

AIKIN: No she ain't.

(TANA *lifts her dress, revealing a thong.*)

MONTY: Tana Weed, you dirty little ho.

(AIKIN *sings and dances to a bit of the "Thong Song."*)

MONTY: That boyfriend of yours ask you to shave it yet?

TANA: What boyfriend.

MONTY: Oh, she thinks she's slick. I heard you on the phone with him, Tana.

AIKIN: She's too stupid to have a boyfriend.

TANA: He ain't my boyfriend.

MONTY: Oh yeah? Who is he then?

TANA: A friend.

MONTY: Who is a boy.

(MONTY *approaches* TANA, *wrestles her cell phone away from her.*)

MONTY: What's your passcode?

TANA: Why?

MONTY: So I can unlock your fuckin' phone!

TANA: I forgot it.

(MONTY *tosses* TANA*'s phone to* AIKIN, *who catches it.* MONTY *grabs* TANA *by her hair, lifts* TANA *off the ground, and slams her face into the refrigerator, bloodying her mouth and nose. This is a brutal, violent act.*)

MONTY: Now tell me your fuckin' password, Tana, or I swear to Christ and Crisco I'll snatch you baldheaded.

TANA: One-zero-two-zero.

(MONTY *releases* TANA.)

(AIKIN *enters* TANA*'s code, unlocks the phone, tosses it back to* MONTY.)

(TANA *lurches, then crosses to her brother, sits beside him, holding her nose.*)

MONTY: *(Studying the phone)* Looks like she's been texting you, Dothan. A big long text… Long as a fuckin' lagoon. Jesus… You in love with your brother, Tana? …What's this boy's real name?

TANA: Why?

MONTY: Cuz I asked you, that's why!

TANA: We ain't even related.

MONTY: Yeah, you're lucky we ain't related! Lucky as a four-leaf-fuckin' clover on top of a birthday cake. Usin' your brother's name, tryin' to be slick!

PIN: Just tell her, Tana.

TANA: Debo.

MONTY: Debo! What the fuck kinda name is Debo?!

AIKIN: Sounds like a retard to me.

MONTY: You lovin' on a retard, Tana?

AIKIN: One of those slow-footed drum fish retards.

MONTY: He's prolly got the diabetes.

AIKIN: He's prolly got the diabetes.

MONTY: He's prolly got the diabetes.

AIKIN: He's prolly got the diabetes.

TANA: Can I have that back please?

MONTY: *(Reading from the text now)* Hey, Boo… *(To* TANA*)* He calls you fuckin' Boo?

TANA: Please don't read that.

MONTY: *(Barreling on)* Is it hot there? …Hot as Hades… *(To* TANA*)* What do you know about Hades? You don't know the first thing about Hell, girl?

(Suddenly, PIN *rises, somewhat inexplicably.)*

PIN: There's this story in the Bible where God turns this donkey into a glass of milk. And the milk gets drunk up by a mountain goat and the mountain goat burps it onto a toad that gets swallowed by Chewbacka before he became a famous actor. FREEZE THE MACHINE!

(PIN, *who has managed to confuse* MONTY, *snatches the phone from her, runs out.*)

MONTY: Pin! Get back here!

AIKIN: He ain't goin' far.

MONTY: Thick-headed ape.

(MONTY *paces, seethes, crosses to the fridge, opens it, removes a box of fast food chicken, crosses to* TANA, *thrusts it at her.*)

MONTY: Go give this to my mother.

(TANA *starts to exit.*)

MONTY: Hey!

(TANA *stops. She thrusts her shoes into her chest.*)

MONTY: Put some fuckin' shorts on.

(TANA *exits with the chicken and her shoes.*)

(MONTY *reaches into the fridge, removes* TANA*'s red sunglasses, puts them on.*)

(MONTY *sings a lullaby, leads* AIKIN *to a distant place in the earth where she attaches medical tubing to his port and takes his blood. The others sing along. The members of the* LOST CHOIR *travel during the song. When* MONTY *encounters them, they either avert her eyes or bow down to her.*)

MONTY: *(Singing)*
River children walk the levee

ALL: *(Singing)*
Watch the water
Watch the water

MONTY: *(Singing)*
River children banks are heavy

ALL: *(Singing)*
Watch the water
Watch the water

MONTY: (*Singing*)
River children
Cast your poles right

ALL: (*Singing*)

Watch the water
Watch the water

MONTY: (*Singing*)
River children
Shade the sunlight

ALL: (*Singing*)
Watch the water
Watch the water
Catch them crappie
Please be happy
No more cryin'
Tears are dryin'

MONTY: (*Singing*)
River children go to sleep now
Watch the water
Watch the water
River children
Chase that dream down
Watch the water
Watch the water

(MONTY *uses an empty jar to collect the blood that she lets from* AIKIN.)

(*A basement*)

(MONTY's *mother,* DUMPTRUCK LORNA, *played by the Wolf, sits in an ancient La-Z-Boy, sunk deep into its depths, a T V on the floor in front of her, which plays "Judge Judy", the sound muted. In her lap she holds a sack of flour. Beside the La-Z-Boy, a dim standing lamp, an oxygen tank. There is a circle of flour around the La-Z-Boy.*)

(TANA *approaches. She is now wearing her sketchers and shorts under her dress. Her face is still bloody.*)

TANA: Hello, Mrs Maloney.

LORNA: Who's that?

TANA: Tana Weed.

LORNA: Tana who?

TANA: Weed.

LORNA: You here to read the meter?

TANA: No.

LORNA: Whathcu want then?

TANA: I'm just bringin' you food.

LORNA: Do I know you?

TANA: I'm Dothan Weed's sister.

LORNA: I have no idea who that is.

TANA: He goes with your daughter.

LORNA: Which one?

TANA: Monty.

LORNA: Monty Mae's got a boyfriend? That bony little slut? How long they been together?

TANA: A while.

LORNA: That's funny. That's damn near hilarious... Is he fuckin' her proper?

TANA: I don't know.

LORNA: Well you should. What's your brother do?

TANA: He...sorta plays music.

LORNA: Disco sucks.

TANA: It ain't disco.

LORNA: Dirty disco. You get the Chlamydia listenin' to that crapola. He in a band?

TANA: Not really.

LORNA: What're they called, the Gaylords?

TANA: He was in the Army.

LORNA: The Army Band ain't so bad. I heard 'em once. They played Lucy in the Sky with Dynamite. You know that one, right? *(Singing)* Lucy in the Sky with Dynamite…

TANA: He didn't play in the Army Band he was just in the Army.

LORNA: He go over to the Middle East?

TANA: Yeah, he got back two years ago.

LORNA: Was he discharged honorably?

TANA: I don't know. He still gets a monthly.

LORNA: Well, did he at least bring you back a souvenir? I hear they got good salad dressing over there. Gasoline and salad dressing… He kill anybody? Cuz once you do that it's pretty much over.

(Again, TANA doesn't answer.)

LORNA: So you got my chicken?

TANA: Yes ma'am.

LORNA: Well bring it here. And watch out for the cat shit.

(TANA approaches her, covering her mouth and nose from the smell.)

LORNA: Come closer. Don't be skeert.

TANA: I ain't.

LORNA: Yes you are. I can smell it on you.

(TANA moves closer, offers the box of chicken. LORNA takes it. TANA scuffs part of the flour circle.)

LORNA: You just scuffed up my circle!

TANA: Sorry.

LORNA: Goddamnit! Now you gotta fix it. Here.

(LORNA *hands the sack of flour to* TANA. TANA *attempts to patch up the scuffed section.*)

LORNA: Make sure you go all the way 'round now. Clean lines. All the way 'round. No squiggles. I can't stand scuffs and I can't stand squiggles!

(TANA *carefully sprinkles flour on the circle, moving slowly around its perimeter.*)

LORNA: This better be a three-piece. That bitch forgets about me.

TANA: She didn't today.

LORNA: Little fucker crawled outta me like a thief. Crawled out and never looked back. (*She considers the box.*) You didn't take none, did you?

TANA: No, ma'am.

(*Nothing is said for a moment. Only Judge Judy*)

LORNA: Old Judy's got 'em confused again… She been at it for almost twenty years. She usually gets it right. Once in a while she screws the pooch, but she's only human… What happened to your face?

TANA: I fell.

LORNA: Into what? A menstrual cramp?

(TANA *completes the circle.*)

LORNA: You know, sometimes if they don't get Judy's hair right she starts to look like George Washinmachine? They should fix that… How old are you anyway?

TANA: Sixteen.

LORNA: Jesus Christmas! You screwin' yet?

TANA: Yes.

LORNA: You must not know why they call me
Dumptruck Lorna. I can smell a fucked pussy a mile
away. You still smell like peaches. When you start
screwin' make sure you get on the birth control, you
hear me?

TANA: Yes ma'am.

LORNA: Babies don't just pop outta birthday cakes…
Switch over to my pong game, willya?

(TANA *crosses to a console in front of the T V, flips a switch.
The old-school video game, Pong, comes on the screen. It's
monotonous, a child's game. She crosses back to* LORNA,
offers her the bag of flour.)

TANA: Here's your flour.

LORNA: Keep it.

TANA: I don't need no flour.

LORNA: People start messin' with you all you gotta do is
make a circle with that flour and step inside the circle.

TANA: Then what happens?

LORNA: You disappear.

TANA: Where do you go?

LORNA: Once I wound up at The Piggly Wiggly. Right
in Aisle Seven. Paper goods and Kleenex. Another time
I appeared in a meadow with dragonflies all around
me. Dragonflies big as birds. Purple, red, butane blue…
Just make sure you close the circle. And I would keep
that in the fridge. It works best when it's cold.

TANA: Thanks, Mrs Maloney.

LORNA: You see my daughter, tell her I want the three-
piece next time.

(TANA *exits.*)

(DOTHAN *enters the kitchen with a child's toy drum,
approaches the refrigerator, opens it, places the toy drum*

inside, closes the door, backs up, anticipation something extraordinary.)

(MONTY enters, unseen.)

MONTY: Do you love me, Dothan?

(DOTHAN turns to MONTY, nods.)

MONTY: You'd do anything for me, right?

(DOTHAN nods.)

MONTY: We livin' the dream, ain't it?

(DOTHAN nods again, starts to approach the refrigerator.)

MONTY: Come here, sweetheart.

(DOTHAN turns, crosses to MONTY. She touches the Arabic characters tattooed on his chest.)

MONTY: You did spectacular things over there, didn't you? I bet you made one helluva beautiful mess.

(DOTHAN starts to say something, stops.)

(MONTY attaches medical tubing to his port, lets blood from his arm as they exit.)

(Later)

(The sounds of crickets, treefrogs, cicadas. Heat pressing down)

(TANA enters the kitchen, puts the sack of flour in the not-cold fridge, shuts the door. PIN appears.)

PIN: Hey.

TANA: *(A bit startled)* Hey.

PIN: You okay?

TANA: I'm fine.

PIN: Your nose.

TANA: What about it?

PIN: Is it busted?

TANA: I don't know.

PIN: Do it hurt?

TANA: What do you think?

PIN: You should get some ice on that.

TANA: That thing don't even get cold enough to make ice. *(She looks around, vigilant.)*

PIN: Don't worry, we're alone.

TANA: Why would I be worried?

PIN: No, you're right.

TANA: Are *you* worried about somethin'?

PIN: No... Should I be?

TANA: I can't speak your mind for you, Pin.

*(*PIN *stands there, confused.)*

TANA: You always need someone to tell you what your thinkin'.

PIN: I do?

TANA: You know you do. You're like a little boy. *(She begins picking up, places all of* DOTHAN's *discarded toys in a crate.)* Where are they, anyway?

PIN: Down by the river.

TANA: Doin' what?

PIN: I don't know. Plannin' stuff.

TANA: What kinda stuff?

PIN: The kinda stuff that requires plannin'.

TANA: Why aren't you with 'em?

PIN: Cuz I'm not.

TANA: That's not a answer.

PIN: Cuz I'm here.

TANA: They're prolly lookin' for you.

PIN: So?

TANA: So you're prolly in deep shit.

PIN: Please don't say that word.

TANA: Shit shit shit shit shit shit shit shit shit shit—

(PIN *punches himself in the thigh. Hard)*

TANA: *(Sharply)* Stop that! …I ain't no little kid no more.

PIN: I know.

TANA: So I can say any word I want.

(PIN *produces her* TANA's *cell pone, starts to say something.)*

TANA: What.

(PIN *says nothing.)*

TANA: Just say what you gotta say.

PIN: Do you love him?

TANA: Pin.

PIN: He don't even know you, Tana.

TANA: Yes he does.

PIN: *(Holding up her cell phone)* This ain't knowin' somebody. This is a fantasy.

TANA: I met him.

PIN: No you didn't.

TANA: Yes I did.

PIN: Where?

TANA: At the little jetty behind the blood bank.

PIN: That's a doggone lie, Tana, and you know it's a doggone lie. That jetty ain't even there no more.

TANA: Well, it used to be.

PIN: Two godforsaken years ago!

TANA: You just can't accept it.

PIN: You really think you got somethin' with him?

TANA: Yes.

PIN: Based on what exactly?

TANA: Based on how he makes me feel.

PIN: How does he make you feel?

TANA: You really want me to answer that?

PIN: Yes.

TANA: He makes me feel special.

PIN: That's crazy.

TANA: Why am I even talkin' to you.

(Beat)

PIN: So you just gonna up and run off to some dumb-ass kid?

TANA: He ain't dumb.

PIN: How do you know?

TANA: Cuz he passed high school, that's how I know. That's mor'n I can say about you. And he knows cars. And he's startin' community college in the fall.

PIN: That don't mean shit.

TANA: To me it do. He knows how to fix air conditioners, too.

PIN: I can do that.

TANA: You can't even fix that damn fridge.

PIN: Cuz they don't make the parts for it no more... At least let me help you.

TANA: Help me how.

PIN: I got money.

TANA: What money? Runnin' them hurricane flowers with Aikin?

PIN: I'm not doin' that no more, Tana, I swear.

TANA: Since when?

PIN: For a while now. I been clearin' fields for Tiny Ramada on the weekends. That's why my hands is so torn up. See? *(Showing his palms)* I been savin' money.

TANA: Monty know you're doin' that?

PIN: No.

TANA: You better hope she don't find out.

PIN: I ain't afraida her.

TANA: Well you should be.

(A tense silence)

PIN: Sometimes I can't feel my face, Tana.

TANA: It's the heat.

PIN: No it's you. My face goes away. And when I'm near you my hands stop workin'. See? *(He holds his hands up to show her.)*

TANA: That's prolly from all that field clearin.

PIN: But my mouth too.

TANA: What about it?

PIN: I can't talk right. I think I know what to say but then…

TANA: Then what.

PIN: Donkeys… Spaceships… Cheddar cheese… See what I mean? Feels like my teeth are fallin' out.

TANA: Are they?

PIN: No.

TANA: Well, there you go.

(Beat)

PIN: I love you, Tana.

TANA: No you don't.

PIN: I do, doggonnit!

TANA: You stink!

PIN: Bad?

TANA: I can smell you from here.

(PIN smells himself.)

TANA: You smell like a animal. Did you shit your pants again?

PIN: No.

TANA: Smells like you did.

PIN: Maybe a little bit.

(Beat)

PIN: Did you hear me? I said I love you… I want to take care of you. Like in a old-fashioned way.

(TANA takes the dirty rag out of the house.)

PIN: I read them texts, Tana! It ain't gonna be easy gettin' outta here! Especailly now that the trainbridge fell.

TANA: I'ma catch a bus.

PIN: What bus?

TANA: The one in Welton.

PIN: Do you even know how far that is?

TANA: It's twenty-three miles.

PIN: And how you plannin' on gettin' there?

TANA: I don't know. I'm just gonna do it.

PIN: You gonna grow wings and fly?

TANA: I'ma cross the river.

PIN: How? You know you can't swim it. Current's too strong. And you swim like a girl.

TANA: Then get me a boat.

PIN: Oh for fucksake, Tana. You don't know how to paddle a boat.

TANA: Just get me one.

PIN: What kind?

TANA: Whatever'll get me across.

PIN: You don't paddle it right you'll get caught in the crosscurrent. Wind up in Tunica or Starkville or some fuckin' place.

TANA: Then that's the chance I'll take.

PIN: When do you need it for?

TANA: Tonight.

PIN: Goddamn *tonight*?

TANA: So you'll do it?

PIN: Fuck my face with a donkey dick.

TANA: Will you or not?

PIN: What are you gonna do for me?

TANA: What do you want?

PIN: Can I have a kiss?

TANA: No.

PIN: I'll give you forty dollars.

TANA: I don't want your money, Pin.

PIN: But you'll take Debo's money. *(He drops to his knees, attacks the earth.)*

TANA: Stop that!

(PIN stops.)

PIN: Can I at least get a hug?

(TANA *approaches* PIN. *He remains on his knees. They hug. He presses his head to her midriff. She holds her breath.*)

PIN: I love you so much, Tana… You know I'd do anything for you.

TANA: Then get me that boat.

PIN: We best get a river rope, too. In case the boat don't work out.

(TANA *breaks from the hug.*)

TANA: Can I have my phone back?

(PIN *hands* TANA *the cell phone.* AIKIN *enters. He is edgy, a bit feral.*)

(PIN *reaches down, picks up the heavy length of chain he'd been plopping in the dirt earlier, wraps it around his fist.*)

AIKIN: (*To* PIN) Monty's lookin' for you.

(TANA *grabs the crate of discarded toys, hands it to* PIN *in an attempt to defuse the fight.*)

(PIN *exits with his chain and the crate of toys.*)

(AIKIN *stares at* TANA, *draws very close to her, then crosses to the refrigerator, reaches on top of it, presses play on the portable C D player. She moves quickly to the C D player, but he points at her and shakes his head, stopping her dead in her tracks. The following song plays. It's a male singer-songwriter's voice and a simple acoustic guitar.*)

Come ride with me
on purple horses
that run in fields
so soft and new
My purple heart
turns black without you
your purple lips
untried and true

(DEBO *appears as a vision, sings the rest of the song. The* LOST CHOIR *sings backup.* TANA *is swept up in her vision, she sings along to the background parts.*)

I say your name
On purple mountains
draw your face
On purple walls
Let's run away
to crazy places
with purple rocks
and waterfalls
I bathe you in
the purple water
I kiss the deep dark dreams
in your eyes
We'll take it slow
through purple valleys
behold the sunsets there
starry skies
They'll never know
our purple forest
Where we'll sleep, sleep, sleep
oh, we'll sleep
I bathe you in
the purple water
I kiss the deep dark dreams in your eyes
So let's go find our purple—

(AIKIN *stops the C D.*)

(DEBO *freezes just as he is about to enter the perimeter of chairs.*)

AIKIN: You like that song?

TANA: Yes.

AIKIN: That ain't no radio song. Somebody gave it to you… That retard boy gave you that song. I'm right, ain't it.

TANA: Do you like it?

AIKIN: Not really. The voice has a sickness.

TANA: But there's a sweetness in it, too.

AIKIN: I wouldn't listen to it too much.

TANA: Why not?

AIKIN: Cuz when a song like that starts livin' inside you it turns you like the trichinoma. You wind up widda heart fungus.

(DEBO *recedes into the darkness.*)

(AIKIN *crouches over a flower, fights his addiction.*)

TANA: You're gonna make yourself sick eatin' all those.

AIKIN: Ever had one?

TANA: No.

AIKIN: Then what do you know about what one of these do to a body?

TANA: But you ain't eatin' just one.

AIKIN: How you know how many I eat?

TANA: Cuz I see you.

AIKIN: You be countin', huh.

(TANA *doesn't deny this.*)

AIKIN: They just flowers. Ain't you the least bit curious?

TANA: There's drugs in 'em.

AIKIN: They don't be puttin' drugs in the doggone flowers.

TANA: No one's puttin' drugs in 'em—they just grow that way. They make your mind weak.

AIKIN: But that's where you're wrong, Tana. They make it strong. They make it see things.

TANA: They make you shiftless. Like everyone else in this godforsaken place.

AIKIN: I eat these flowers and I don't got to go nowhere. Cuz I'm already travelin'. Like they do in movies.

TANA: Where do you travel to?

AIKIN: I been to the circus. I been to a rodeo. I been to this place where all these birds talk like men.

TANA: What were they sayin'.

AIKIN: You really wanna know?

TANA: Yes.

AIKIN: They said there's this place we go when we die. It's underneath everything. Under the mud. Under the bentonite mines.
Deeper'n water.
It's a big sprawlin' house. Kinda like a castle. And all these little kids is there, sittin' on the floor. And they moufs is saggin' open like they wonderin' about shit. And inside each of they moufs is another little kid. And they moufs is open, too. And inside they moufs is another little kid. Small as a flickerdill. Fleafly small. And on and on like that, forever and ever into perpitude.

TANA: Is that sposed to be Hell?

AIKIN: I think it's just a house.
(He begins trembling.)

TANA: Why are you shakin'?

AIKIN: I ain't shakin'.

TANA: It's ninety-four degrees and you're shakin' like a leaf.

AIKIN: You the one shakin!

TANA: *(Careful)* Okay.

AIKIN: I move anyway I want. If I wanna be still I be still. If I wanna dance I dance. If I wanna fly I fly… Can I tell you somefin' else, Tana?

TANA: Okay.

AIKIN: This is real important. You listenin'?

TANA: I'm listenin'.

AIKIN: *Sit down!*

(TANA quickly sits.)

AIKIN: When I eat the flowers I ain't skeert no more. I ain't askeert'a no darkness. I ain't askeert'a no animals. I ain't askeert'a no monsterfishes or God or evils spirits nuther.
The other day I ate four of 'em and I jumped in the river. Right where the train bridge fell to crumplin'. And I swimmed up under the joints of the bridge—the whole mess of it—and I forced myself into the maze of its trickiest parts. I wasn't skeert, Tana. Nope. The drumfish was drummin' and the catfish had they hackles up and them cottonmoufs was slitherin' with the quickness, but I was good. I felted like I coulda breaved water. I coulda drunk up that whole river. And when Aikin came up for air it was cuz he wanted to. His lungs was fulla gold and his heart was silver. You understand what that means, Tana? Aikin came up for air Cuz he wanted to.
(He is drawn to another flower. He moves to it.)
Sometimes the water talks to me, Tana. I walk right up to it and wait for it to teach me things.

TANA: What does it teach you?

AIKIN: About time. And the willfulness of the bluff rocks. How men ain't shit but bodies wigglin'. Bodies wif bones in 'em. Man ain't no better'n a fish or a ramblin'-faced goat. Man ain't barely better'n a tree. The water knows, Tana. That's where we all go in the

end: back to the water. And that's where we come from
in the first place. A belly fulla motherwater. Water's the
smartest thing they is.
(*He considers the flower in his hand.*
You want this one?

(TANA *shakes her head.*)

AIKIN: *(A warning)* When things happen you can't
afford to be skeert.

TANA: What's gonna happen?

(AIKIN *smiles, puts the flower in his mouth, chews.*)

(*A special comes up on* MONTY, *dressed in a sad glittering
outfit. She lip synchs to Miley Cyrus's ballad, "When I
Look at You", conjuring magic lights, a disco ball, using
the entire space for her world class performance. It is
nothing less than breathtaking. The* LOST CHOIR *assists her
throughout.*)

(*When* MONTY *finishes the performance she finds* DOTHAN
across the world, moves to him.)

MONTY: Am I the Queen, Dothan?!

(DOTHAN *nods.*)

MONTY: And you're my King?

(DOTHAN *nods.*)

MONTY: I chose you because you know the terrible
beauty in the world. You have glimpsed the majestic
horrors of things torn asunder. The black orbs of the
unexplained. Fecal-skinned children with the spired
teeth of dragonfish.

(DOTHAN *watches* MONTY *as if she is a distant fire.*)

MONTY: This is our kingdom and we are sovereign to
all.
(*She looks out over her kingdom.*)

We are sovereign to all, Dothan… We are sovereign…
Sovereign….

(Lights fade to black.)

(The WOLF *snaps his fingers and all lights pop to brightness. Once again, the audience is fully exposed.)*

WOLF: The human body contains seven cervical, twelve thoracic, five lumbar, sacral, and coccygeal vertebrae.

(The WOLF *snaps his fingers and two male members of the* LOST CHOIR *assume standing positions on opposite sides of the mound.)*

WOLF: There's also the sternum, the ribs, and the costal cartilages. The skull is made up of eight cranial bones: the occipital, parietal, frontal, temporal, sphenoid, and ethmoid bones. There are fifteen facial bones, which include the nasal bones, the maxillae, the lacrimal, the zygomatic and the palatine, the inferior nasal concha, the vomer, the mandible (one of my favorites), and the hyoid, which is a horseshoe-shaped bone that floats mysteriously in the center of the throat. There is the interior and exterior of the skull. The middle ear has six bones: pairs of malleus, incus, and stapes bones.

(The WOLF *snaps and* MALE CHOIR MEMBER #1 *thrusts his arm out to the side.)*

WOLF: In the upper arm extremity there's the clavicle, the scapula, the humerus, the ulna, and the radius. In each hand there's the carpus, the metacarpus, and the phalanges. The phalanges has a subset of bones called proximal, intermediate, and distal phalanges. The carpal, or wrist, contains many bones. *(quickly)* Scaphoid, lunate, triquetrum, pisiform, trapezium, trapezoid, capitate, and hamate. Sounds like ingredients for a stew, don't it?

(The WOLF *genuflects, snaps.* MALE CHOIR MEMBER #1 *sits on his leg.)*

WOLF: The leg contains important weight-bearing bones. The hipbone comprises the fused ilium, the ishcium and the pubis. There are two of them. The good ole double pubis. I'm pretty sure that's where some essential organs are housed... There's also the pelvis, the femur, the patella, the tibia, and the fibula.

There are twenty-six bones in each foot, fifty-two-total. The tarsus yields pairs of calcaneus or heel bones, taluses, naviculars, medial cuneiforms, intermediate cuneiforms, lateral cuneiforms, and cuboids. I once knew a alligator dealer called Nancy Cuboid, but I digress... Back to the foot, where we still have the metatarsus and those old friendly phalanges: pairs of proximal, intermediate, and distal flanges, much like the hand. And the sesamoid bones. Sesamoid. Sounds a little like a salad dressing, don't it?

(The WOLF *snaps and* MALE CHOIR MEMBER #1 *stands, assumes his original position. The* WOLF *approaches* MALE CHOIR MEMBER #2.)*

WOLF: In the shoulder girdle there are four bones: two clavicles, also known as the collarbones...

(The WOLF *snaps and* MALE CHOIR MEMBER #2 *doubles over, exposing his back.)*

WOLF: And two scapula, also known as the shoulder blades.

(The Wolf snaps and MALE CHOIR MEMBER #2 *stands tall again.)*

WOLF: In the thorax there are twenty-five bones. The sternum or breastbone, is one of them, which is comprised of the gladiolus, the manubrium, and the Xiphoid process. The Xiphoid process is this little bone next to the heart, not even two-fingers away. The heart is not a bone so I'm not even gonna broach that subject. The heart is a...

(A light turns on in LORNA's *apartment, revealing a fish mounted to her paneled wall.)*

WOLF: Fish!

(The light shuts off.)

WOLF: But just to be clear, the sternum only counts as one bone, with these attendant smaller pieces serving as skeletal acolytes, if you will.
And lastly…

(The WOLF *snaps again.* MALE CHOIR MEMBER #2 *inhales mightily, lifts his elbows, exposing his ribs.)*

WOLF: …there are the ribs. Two sets of twelve.

(From his pocket, the WOLF *produces a lollipop, inserts it in* MALE CHOIR MEMBER #2's *mouth.)*

WOLF: There's an old wives' tale involving a greedy lady who took a rib from her man to make her somehow particular. But that's just an old wives' tale. Cuz I'm here to tell you, that the girl sittin' in this chair here has twelve ribs. I know she does. I counted 'em myself. Pulled 'em right outta the mud with the crayfish and dragonfly wings. *(Points to an audience member)* You were there, weren't you? Didn't you count 'em with me? No? I must be mistaken—I coulda sworn that was you. *(Point to another audience member)* Weren't you there, too? Yes, you were, weren't you… A dozen ribs. *(He addresses another audience member.)* That's right, you got a dozen of 'em, too. And so do you, pretty lady. And you, and you, and you, friend. A dozen ribs. That's like eggs, ain't it? Eggs, oysters, donuts…
These bones were in the river. Yep, they settled in the bottom of your cold watery belly. But whose are they? Are they the bones of a bentonite miner? Or some drowned fisherman who ran into a patch of confounding water? Or a stranger on his way to other places? Or are they the bones of a girl? Y'all prolly

know better'n I do. Cuz a river has a memory too,
yes it certainly does. I think a river such as this one
remembers just about everything there is.
But before we thrust ourselves headlong into the
inevitable, let's hold tight for a second.

(As directed by the WOLF, MALE CHOIR MEMBER #1 *and
#2 exit.)*

WOLF: Time is a tricky old sow, ain't she? She'll root
around on her belly. She'll bury her snout in just
about anything and fatten-up. Sometimes she'll
even perambulate through the muck ass-backwards,
her hocks peripatetic and contrary, like she forgot
somethin'. The Great Sow of Time, gruntin' through the
slopyard.
Now the last thing in the world anyone wants to be
is sentimental, but there was this one day, this one
very *special significant unforgettable extraordinary* and
treasured day when everything was right... The sun
was right... The water was right... The breeze was
right. Bees were doin' somersaults. Dragonflies were
vectorin' around. It was as perfect a day in recent
memory. Perfect as puppy piss and puppy piss is
as perfect a thing there is. It was the kinda day that
coulda changed everything. It mighta been the best
day of Tana Weed's life. So let's alight on this day for a
minute, shall we? Cuz no matter how bad things get,
everyone gets at least one day there where stuff looks
downright possible. Objects attain a gilded edge. The
sun marbles the skin of the water. The trees look plump
and green. Even the fish start to look heroic. *(To an
audience member)* I'm right, ain't it, neighbor?
So let's go back there, shall we? *(To* TANA*)* Tana?

(The WOLF *offers* TANA *the top of the mound. She removes
her dress, revealing her cutoff shorts and a cheap bikini top.
A sunhat flies in, which the he catches and places on her*

*head. He also offers her a handkerchief, which she uses to
wipe the blood from her nose and mouth.)*

WOLF: So this is over two years ago. Tana is alone,
laying back on an old rickety dock, lookin' out on the
water, lost in thought, sunnin' herself in the manner
that certain young ladies do, when a young man
approaches on a skiff. He is standin' on it, using a long
pole to maneuver.

*(DEBO appears outside the perimeter of the audience,
standing on a skiff, using a pole to navigate.)*

(The WOLF stands beside the fridge, watches.)

(During this scene, PIN quietly builds a boat in the corner.)

DEBO: Hey.

TANA: Hey.

DEBO: Pretty stretch of river you got here.

TANA: It ain't my river.

DEBO: Whose is it?

TANA: God's...the Devil's...the Great Maker of
Miracles and Waterways.

DEBO: You okay?

TANA: I'm fine.

DEBO: That dock don't look fine.

TANA: This old thing's all right.

DEBO: It looks like it's about to collapse.

TANA: Looks can be deceivin'... Why, you worried
I'm gonna fall in? You sposed to be some kinda river
guard?

DEBO: Maybe.

TANA: "Maybe" ain't no real word. Maybe's one of
those words like snagtag. Or yuktimmytoo.

DEBO: I'd wager that it's in the dictionary.

TANA: You would, would you?

DEBO: Maybe? Indeed I would. I'd bet my cutthroat boat here that it's classified as an adverb.

TANA: If maybes were babies we'd all be on welfare.

DEBO: Are you on welfare?

TANA: Maybe I am.

DEBO: You're too young to be on welfare.

TANA: You don't know spit.

DEBO: How old are you—fifteen?

(TANA *is inscrutable.*)

DEBO: Fourteen?

TANA: You always go around talkin' to jailbait?

(DEBO*'s clearly charmed. He moves his boat around.*)

DEBO: What's your name, anyway?

TANA: Tana.

DEBO: Tana… That rhymes with banana.

TANA: Rhymes with a whole lotta things.

DEBO: You live around here?

TANA: I might.

DEBO: What's this place called?

TANA: The Maybe Place.

DEBO: Maybe, U S A?

TANA: That's right.

DEBO: I thought Maybe wasn't a real word.

TANA: Maybe this ain't no real place.

DEBO: *You* seem real.

TANA: Do I?

DEBO: Real as this water.

TANA: Maybe I'm a mermaid.

DEBO: Mermaids don't have such pretty feet.

(This causes TANA *to blush. She might wiggle her toes.)*

DEBO: I was just over in Tunica.

TANA: You ain't from Tunica.

DEBO: I'm from Benton.

TANA: Never hearda Benton.

DEBO: It's in Illinois. Southern tip of the state. Franklin County.

TANA: Illinois, huh?

DEBO: Yes, ma'am. Land of Lincoln.

TANA: Don't ma'am me. I ain't no cafeteria worker. Ma'am my ass.
(Beat)
So what's in Tunica? Besides a buncha white trash lowlife meth heads in broken-down cars.

DEBO: Um, casinos… My dad's over at the Harrah's right now.

TANA: Well this ain't nothin' like Tunica.

DEBO: Is it better or worse?

TANA: Depends on what you're lookin' for. We don't got no casinos.

DEBO: From the looks of it you don't got much of anything 'round here. Except maybe that old train bridge over there.

TANA: Ain't been a train on that bridge since I been alive. They keep sayin' it's gonna collapse any minute now. It's condemned.

DEBO: I bet people drink on that bridge.

TANA: They do a lot more 'n that.

DEBO: Like what?

TANA: Drink, smoke, fuck each other silly…disappear.

DEBO: Where do they disappear to?

TANA: Nobody knows for sure. Away from here.

DEBO: And those are some peculiar lookin' blackbirds.

TANA: Them ain't blackbirds.

DEBO: What are they?

TANA: Bats.

DEBO: *Bats*?

TANA: Fruit bats.

DEBO: *Seriously*?

TANA: You don't got fruit bats up in Benton?

DEBO: No. Are they poisonous?

TANA: If you get bit you gotta get a shot.

DEBO: Fruit bats?

TANA: Don't worry, they ain't gonna mess witchu.

DEBO: …You like my skiff? Solo Microskiff. Pretty crisp, ain't it? …You wanna join me? …You do, I can tell.

TANA: That thing's too small.

DEBO: There's plenty of room.

TANA: You sposed to be standin' on it like that?

DEBO: The Solo Microskiff's built for standin'.

TANA: Why, so you can act like a waiter?

DEBO: So you can flyfish.

TANA: Evenin', sir, can I take your order.

DEBO: Tonight's special is grilled halibut.

TANA: You're a halibut.

(The WOLF *trains a flashlight on* DOTHAN, *who is outside the perimeter of the chairs.)*

WOLF: Right around this time—it mighta been this very day, in fact—on the other side of the planet, Private First Class Dothan Weed was on a scout mission, on the outskirts of Kabul. His tour of duty had been relatively uneventful up until now and he'd been ordered by his lieutenant to go ahead of his unit a few miles and report back.

*(*DOTHAN *steps out of the light, into darkness. The* WOLF *turns the flashlight off, moves away.)*

DEBO: Tana, huh?

TANA: That's my name, don't wear it out.

DEBO: What's your last name?

TANA: Why?

DEBO: Cuz you might be the prettiest thing I've ever seen and after I float away from here when I think of you I'd like to know the full melody that is the song that is your name.

TANA: Listen to you.

DEBO: I just know a particular kinda vision when I see one.

TANA: You better be careful. There's all kindsa snakes in that water. Cottonmouths.

DEBO: Snakes don't bother me.

TANA: The snakes around here are in cahoots with the bats. Cottonmouths with sickled teeth. They'll slither up on you with the quickness.

(The WOLF *enters the space, once again training his flashlight on* DOTHAN, *who has traveled to another position behind the audience.)*

WOLF: After about a mile, Private First Class Dothan weed happened upon the strangest thing: a steer. A majestic, quarter-ton, prolifically-horned steer, just standin' there, grazin'. Chimerical and solitary. Somehow it had gotten away from its herd.

(DOTHAN *moves out of the light and into darkness. The* WOLF *shuts off the flashlight, disappears.*)

DEBO: You should ask me my name.

TANA: Why?

DEBO: Cuz it's polite.

TANA: Who said I was polite.

DEBO: Okay then. Nice talkin' to you, Tana whatever-your-name-is.

TANA: Where you goin'?

(DEBO *continues moving away.*)

TANA: Wait.

DEBO: Enjoy your evenin'.

TANA: Hey!

(DEBO *stops.*)

TANA: Don't go… Stay and talk to me.

(DEBO *returns.*)

TANA: What's your name, anyway?

DEBO: Debo.

TANA: *Debo*?

DEBO: Yeah, Debo.

TANA: That don't rhyme with a damn thing.

DEBO: It rhymes with "placebo".

TANA: Palebo ain't no word.

DEBO: Placebo. Yes it is.

TANA: What's it mean?

DEBO: I don't know, but it's a word. I think it's medical.

TANA: What kinda name is Debo?

DEBO: One that you should write over your heart.

TANA: I should, huh?

(DEBO *produces a back Sharpie pen, tosses it to* TANA.)

DEBO: D-E-B-O. Right over that most vital muscle.

TANA: And what's that gonna do?

DEBO: It might just change your life.

TANA: What makes you think I wanna change my life?

DEBO: You ain't happy.

TANA: I'm not, huh.

DEBO: I can tell.

TANA: How so?

DEBO: Your eyes.

TANA: What about 'em?

DEBO: Ever seen a blob fish?

TANA: No.

DEBO: Saltwater fish from Australia.

TANA: You been to Australia?

DEBO: No, but I seen pictures of blob fishes on the Internet. Saddest eyes you've ever seen.

TANA: So you're sayin' I look like a doggone fish?

DEBO: I didn't say that.

TANA: I think you mighta just called me a blob fish.

DEBO: I just mean you got sad eyes. Even from here I can see that...I could make `em happy.

TANA: What do you know?

DEBO: A lot.

TANA: You don't know squiggity-squat.

DEBO: I know what I know, I just go with the flow.

TANA: You think you're slick.

DEBO: That's right. I'm Slick Rick on the re-quest line. I'd like to know your name and your zodiac sign.

(Beat)

TANA: Is Debo a nickname?

DEBO: Sort of.

TANA: It's your hip-hop name?

DEBO: No.

TANA: What's your real name?

DEBO: Beauregard.

TANA: I like Debo better. Beauregard sounds like a furniture store.

(The WOLF *trains his flashlight on* DOTHAN, *who has traveled.)*

WOLF: So Private First Class Dothan Weed approaches the steer. He draws very close. Close enough to where he can smell the sharp foul musk of its hide and peer into its eyes. Probably the deepest brownest most mysterious eyes he's ever seen. These are the kind of eyes that can teach a man that he is no greater than the beast he is beholding. That the various tissues that comprise its flanks and loins are forged from the same muck found in the anatomical particulars of lunatics and saints. And then Private First Class Dothan Weed raises his automatic weapon to the steer's head, just below the left horn, and fires two rounds into the soft gelatinous loaf that is its brain.

*(*DOTHAN *stares directly into the flashlight beam. The* WOLF *turns it off, crosses back to the fridge.)*

DEBO: How long you been sittin' there?

TANA: Maybe like a hour. Maybe my whole life.

DEBO: What do you do for fun around here?

TANA: What do you do in Benton?

DEBO: Fish. Play baseball. Mess around with cars.

TANA: You don't got no car.

DEBO: Yes I do.

TANA: What kind?

DEBO: Two-thousand-thirteen Honda Civic Hatchback. I'm about to put a new engine in it. With a Full Race intake manifold and B D L seventy-two millimeter throttle body.

TANA: Your just sayin' words.

DEBO: No I ain't. I'ma drag it up in Aledo. You know where that is?

TANA: Some place in your mind.

DEBO: Aledo's up by Chicago.

TANA: Whipdeedo.

DEBO: You've never been to Chicago… You prolly haven't been anywhere… You should come visit me.

TANA: I should, huh?

DEBO: Yes.

TANA: You'll take me for a spin in your 2013 Honda Civic Hatchback?

DEBO: I most certainly will.

TANA: I can't.

DEBO: Why not?

TANA: Cause I'm waitin' for someone to come home.

DEBO: Boyfriend?

TANA: My brother. He's over in Afghanistan.

DEBO: You miss him?

(TANA *nods*.)

DEBO: What's his name?

TANA: Dothan.

DEBO: When's he comin' back?

TANA: Supposably in a few weeks. If he don't get killed.

DEBO: He won't get killed.

TANA: How do you know?

DEBO: Gut feeling. He'll prolly be happy to see you.

TANA: He better be. He better cry.

DEBO: Your parents must be excited.

TANA: They ain't around.

DEBO: Where'd they go?

TANA: My dad died. Got caught in the mines.

DEBO: What about your mom?

TANA: She left when we was little. I think she might be a stewardess or somethin'.

DEBO: My dad's a farmer. And my mother teaches second grade.

(*The* WOLF *appears*.)

WOLF: (*To the audience*) Ain't this somethin'? Didn't I tell you? A day unlike any other. I have a mind to restart this scene from its very beginning. But that might verge on indulgences we simply can't afford right now. No, no, no, we simply cannot afford those at this time.

DEBO: So do you got a boyfriend or what?

TANA: No.

DEBO: Well, you do now.

TANA: Shut up!

DEBO: I'm serious.

TANA: You don't even know me!

DEBO: But I want to.

TANA: I might have fangs.

DEBO: Sickled like a cottonmouth?

TANA: Might have 'em in the wrong places.

DEBO: I'm at a loss as to how I'm sposed to respond to that.

TANA: "I'm at a loss as to how I'm sposed to respond to that."

DEBO: Come here.

TANA: Why?

DEBO: So I can write on your arm.

TANA: Whatchu gonna write on it?

DEBO: My phone number.

TANA: How 'bout I give you mine instead?

DEBO: Whatever's clever.

(TANA *stands with the Sharpie.* DEBO *enters the circle of chairs, offers his arm. She writes on it.*)

DEBO: What're them marks on your arm?

(TANA *hides her arms.*)

TANA: It's from givin' blood.

DEBO: You get paid for that?

TANA: For the plasma. Nine dollars a pop… Sometimes my brother can't send his pay home.

DEBO: Who watches you?

TANA: I watch myself.

DEBO: Are you hungry?

TANA: Why, do I look skinny?

DEBO: You do.

TANA: In a bad way?

DEBO: No.

TANA: I ate today.

DEBO: What'd you eat?

TANA: You sposed to be some kinda social worker?

DEBO: You should come with me. We got a nice place. Big willow tree in the backyard.

TANA: We got willow trees here.

DEBO: We got dogs too. Blue ticks. Ever seen a bluetick before? Best huntin' dog on the planet.

TANA: Where you from again?

DEBO: Benton, Illinois. George Harrison visited once. You know who he was?

TANA: Was he president?

DEBO: No. He was one of the Beatles.

TANA: That's old people music.

DEBO: Seriously, come with me, Tana.

TANA: I already told you about my brother.

DEBO: So come visit after he gets back.

TANA: Maybe I will. Mister Microskiff. *(She offers the Sharpie.)*

DEBO: Keep that.

TANA: Why?

DEBO: So you can write that name on your heart.

TANA: Beauregard.

DEBO: Debo.

TANA: …D-E-B-…O?

(DEBO *nods, starts to push away.*)

DEBO: Don't give too much of that pretty blood of yours away now. (*He fades into the distance.*)

(DOTHAN *enters the kitchen with a toy, approaches the refrigerator. He opens it, places the toy inside, closes the door, waits. He opens the door. The intense WHOPPING, circular sound of Chinook helicopter blades issues forth. This sound grows. Light blasts out of the refrigerator. When he can no longer stand it, he closes the refrigerator door. The sound ceases.*)

(MONTY, *dressed as a technician from the blood bank, in hospital scrubs, enters the circle of chairs, joins* TANA *at the top of the mound.* TANA *stands.* MONTY *speaks directly to the audience.* TANA *grows weaker throughout the speech.*)

MONTY: Yeah, I knew her. She was a nice girl. Tana Weed had a real purity about her. Tana Weed. You can tell a lot about a person when you're takin' blood from 'em. Is she strong? Is she weak? Does she exhibit iron deficiencies? Does her blood jump? And what does the skin do when the needle gets close? Cuz a needle can get closer than just about anything else there is. Some say a needle gets closer than God can. It gets inside you and God can't do that, Nu-uh. Not even when you invite him in. If you want my opinion I think God is scared about most things. God's got the heart of a earthworm.

When you take blood you also learn about a person's composure. Do they faint? Do they get turned on? Do they start sweatin'? How do they respond to venous pressure? If you lance a artery sometimes they'll go into shock. Now that's real interestin' when that happens. Shock. How one's system stands up to things…

(TANA *falls to the earth, unconscious.* MONTY *snatches her sunhat before* TANA *meets the dirt.* MONTY *strokes* TANA's *hair maternally.*)

MONTY: I have no idea what happened to Tana Weed. It's sad when a pretty girl just disappears into thin air like that. When she gets swallowed by the night. Some say she drowned tryin' to cross the river. Others say she was pulled limb from limb by a pack of wolves. One story has it that she disappeared into a circle of flour. Stories are fun, ain't they?

(MONTY *addresses* PIN, *who has been building a boat.*)

MONTY: Ansel Pinwood, what are you doin'?

PIN: Nothin'.

MONTY: That don't look like nothin' to me. What is that?

PIN: A boat.

MONTY: Now why on God's greasy earth do you need a boat?

PIN: For fishin'.

MONTY: But you fish off the edge of the levee. There's plenty of fish right there. You got sturgeon, crappie, drum fish, trout for days.

PIN: I wanna go further out.

MONTY: Oh, you wanna get you a big one, huh? You want one of them giant catfish. You want a Mekong… So ambitious.

(PIN *continues working.*)

MONTY: Can I ask you a question, Pin?

PIN: Uh-huh?

MONTY: Are you still devoted? Cuz I'm gettin' a keen sense that you been somewhat adrift lately. And now here you are makin' this boat.

PIN: I'm devoted.

MONTY: Prove it.

PIN: How?

(MONTY *produces* TANA*'s Sharpie.*)

MONTY: Write my name over your heart.

(PIN *stares at* MONTY.)

MONTY: I did it.
(*She exposes herself.* "PIN" *is written across her heart.*)
I'm devoted to you. You're right there on my heart.
You're more than family to me. Did you know that,
Pin?

(PIN *is suddenly mesmerized.*)

MONTY: Go on, now.

(PIN *removes his shirt.* MONTY *approaches him, moves very
close. Her proximity renders him very still. He starts to
breathe intensely.*)

MONTY: What happened to your blood port?

PIN: I lost it.

MONTY: You can't just go around losing things, Ansel.

PIN: Sorry, Monty.

MONTY: (*Sweetly*) You need me to do it for you?

(PIN *nods.* MONTY *writes* "MONTY" *over his heart.*)

MONTY: (*Writing*) "M" is for Monty Mae Maloney
and extra thick baloney. "O" is for Oh my god there's
a goddamn crocodile in my kitchen! "N" is for nice
girls and beautiful boys and all the dirty disco toys.
"T" is for two tons of terrible fallin' on the house of
happy. And "Y" is for you and me setting all the baby
dragonfish free.

(MONTY *caresses* PIN. *He falls to his knees. She sets the
Sharpie between his teeth. He bites down.*)

MONTY: Now when we're done here I'm gonna need you to do one more thing for me, okay?

(PIN *nods, delirious, confused, swooning.*)

MONTY: I'm gonna need you to stop makin' that boat. Cuz I'd hate to think that my one and only Ansel Pinwood might get stuck too far out in that piddly little thing, tryin' to wrestle down one of them Mekongs. If you didn't make it back it would make me the saddest girl this side of I-don't-know-what. So please stop makin' that, Pinny-Pin-Pin. Can you do that for me?

PIN: Yes, Monty.

(AIKIN *appears with an axe.*)

MONTY: But just to be safe, I think we should make it easy for you.

(AIKIN *approaches the makeshift boat, whistling "River Children." He brings the axe down onto the makeshift boat with finality.*)

(*Darkness*)

(*The sound of epic snoring.* LORNA's *standing lamp and her Pong game are the only sources of light.*)

(DOTHAN *enters her basement, moving with stealth. He kicks a can.*)

LORNA: Who's that?

(DOTHAN *says nothing, creeps closer.*)

LORNA: That the meter man? I paid that goddamn light bill! Put it in the mail on Tuesday!

(DOTHAN *says nothing.*)

LORNA: Well, speak up! This ain't no libary!

(DOTHAN *slowly approaches.* LORNA *produces a small beauty mirror, holds it up so she can see who is behind her.*)

LORNA: Is that you, Dothan Weed? Ain't you the one
fornicatin' with my daughter. Didn't you just get back
from the goddamn war? Hope it was worth it. All that
fightin' over a little oil… How many sand niggers you
kill? Bet you got at least a dozen of 'em. Am I right?
…Well, speak up, boy! That ain't nothin' to be ashamed
of. I hear killin' people's just like steppin' on cabbages.
You think that's true? …I tried to get Monty Mae
to enlist but she wouldn't have it. I think she's too
goddamn cowardly to go fight in a war. Where is that
little bow-legged slut anyway? I don't know what in
God's lubricious, chlamydia-smeared earth you could
possibly see in her.

(DOTHAN *is suddenly mesmerized by her Pong game.*)

LORNA: What the hell are you lookin' at?

(DOTHAN *covers her mouth, embraces her head, and breaks
her neck. He then moves to her television, disconnects the
console for her Pong game, steals it. He runs out, scurries
home. He enters his house, where* TANA *is asleep, in front
of the refrigerator, in the fetal position, the door open,
lighting her figure. He watches her for a brief moment, opens
his mouth, as if to say something, closes it, then sits with
his Pong game, starts manipulating it, getting lost in its
particulars.*)

(TANA *stirs, sees* DOTHAN.)

TANA: Hey.

(DOTHAN *doesn't respond.*)

TANA: Where'd you get that?

(DOTHAN *starts taking apart the game.*)

TANA: Dothan.

(DOTHAN *turns to* TANA.)

TANA: Where'd you get that, Dothan?

(DOTHAN *just stares at* TANA.)

TANA: Did you take that from somebody's house?

(DOTHAN *turns away.*)

TANA: You can't keep takin' other peoples' property, Dothan. You're gonna get in trouble.

(DOTHAN *continues busying himself with the guts of the game.*)

TANA: I wish you'd say somethin'.

(*No response*)

TANA: You can't just stay like this for the rest of your life.

(*Still nothing*)

TANA: So I wasn't gonna tell you but I'm leavin'... Did you hear me, Dothan? I said I was leavin' and I ain't comin' back.

(TANA *waits for him to respond. She waits a while, but he continues manipulating the game.*)

(*The* WOLF *enters.*)

WOLF: When Private First Class Dothan Weed returned home from his tour of duty in Kabul, his sister baked him a cake. It was a Betty Crocker Super Moist yellow cake with chocolate frosting and it had as many candles as she could possible fit on it.

(TANA *reaches into the refrigerator, produces a cake in a pan.*)

WOLF: Dothan was wearing his dress greens and his hair was cut short and parted neatly on the side and he had a clean shave but somethin' was different. Tana had been waiting for this day for as long as she could remember and when he walked in that door there everything certainly looked right. The candles were lit. Tana was wearing her favorite dress. She'd cleaned the whole house, top to bottom. She even threw two

handfuls of confetti. But he didn't even smile. There
was somethin' different about his eyes. Somethin'
blacker than she remembered. She put the cake down
and embraced her brother. And although his arms
reciprocated the embrace in a classic sense there was
nothin' particularly inspired about it. Tana might have
been huggin' a department store dummy.
After the hug, Dothan Weed dropped his duffle bag
and proceeded to do the strangest thing. He took all his
clothes off. There were many parts to his uniform and
he shed them with a slowness attributed to men of the
clergy. And when he was good and naked, he simply
stood before his sister and pointed to a crude tattoo
that had been carved into the breast over his heart.
And then he said the following:

DOTHAN: I can't find my knee. Is it still there?

TANA: Yeah, it's still there.

WOLF: "I can't find my knee. Is it still there?" "Yeah,
it's still there."
They stood there for along while. All the candles of
the cake burned down to bits. This is the kind of story
that has no clear intended meaning, and therefore
some might think it to be a useless story, an anecdote
without consequence. But the fact of the matter is that
this was the last thing Dothan Weed said to his sister.
And that's a true story. And a true story is always the
best story there is.

(TANA *puts the cake back in the fridge, closes the door,
exits.*)

(*Lights change. It's a cruel, unforgiving, monstrous light.*)

(DOTHAN *removes his headphones. He directs some of the
following to the* WOLF, *who plays along as necessary.*)

DOTHAN: (*To the* WOLF) The sound of Chinooks like
forever monsters. They don't never land, they just keep

circlin' and circlin' like the mind of the world. Soldier,
did you bring the barbecue sauce this time? Cuz that
little girl with the big brown eyes ain't no bigger than
a doll. Them eyes ain't brown they're *shit* brown. Shit
brown eyes and a brain like a turkey turd. But a good
barbecue sauce can turn a flavor in even the nastiest
meat. Secure the perimeter, soldier!

Didn't I tell you already?! Secure the perimeter and
make it dandy, as in Yankee doodle. How many
Afghanis do it take to wash an alligator? How much
Kabuli Palaw do it take to stuff a circus bear? How
much Grad-A American flapjack mix do it take to start
a wafflehouse in Kabul? Did you take that weapon off
a civilian, soldier? Then take it to your truck and get a
move on!

Yes, sir, Company Commander, sir! *(To the Audience)*
He happened upon a steer in the middle of the desert.
Walked up to it and shot it like it was a man, just like
a enemy man. Eyes so brown they go forever, which
is where the water in Hell is. And this is where you
take all the babies after they get laid in the street, you
take 'em to this hellwater and put 'em in it, you don't
even got to wash 'em, you just drop 'em in and wait
for the water to rise up over their little faces. Everyone
gets two nostrils. Even the Afghani babies that get
laid in the street get two little ones. There's a sound
in the body that's like a Chinook sound. If you could
reach inside yourself with your gladdest hand, would
you remove the heart? The heart of that little Afghani
girl wasn't no bigger than a toad, the heart of her
and her mother and her father, who is more animal
than human you can tell cuz he's got rodents running
around in his belly and you can reach inside him and
take his heart out, it ain't no bigger than the fist of that
boy there and don't forget to confiscate his weapon,
too, soldier, yeah, that boy there with the faraway look

on his face, the barefoot one wearing the T-shirt with
LeBron James flying on it, take his weapon off him and
put it on your truck and always make sure to keep a
good bottle of barbecue sauce on your truck cuz you
never know when you might want to barbecue some
little girl and her brother with the funny arm and her
mommy and daddy. It's crazy how the skin sizzles
and pops when you turn it over fire. You clean them
bodies just like a fish, just like a giant walleye you pull
out of a river. Bury the innards in the dirt otherwise
all them wild dogs'll come the ones with the snarly
faces but you can just shoot them too but they're lower
and faster than a man and they will try and bite you.
Infidel! Infidel, infidel, infidel! The word goes in you
like a knife, right into the soft loaves of flesh in your
side, it goes in like a long cold knife that possesses its
own thought and it stays there forever. Forever is that
place inside you where the Chinooks keep whopping,
whop…whop…whop…whop…whop…whop…
whop…whop…whop…whop…whop…whop…
whop…

*(The other members of the ensemble close in on him, turn
into wolves, attack him, removes his heart, eat it, resuscitate
him, dance and celebrate with him, freeze. A young woman
moves through the forest of bodies. He addresses the other
members of the ensemble, who abandon him, one by one, over
the following:)*

DOTHAN: Catch that girl! Yeah that one there! Catch
her and tie her to that pole. Catch that girl, soldier, she
ain't no faster than a sick cat walkin' backwards in a
thunderstorm! Catch that girl! Catch her and secure
her to that pole there and wait for further instruction!
I am your company commander and you will do as I
say! My voice is the voice of God and God's voice is
a whopping Chinook and God's voice is the sound of
dirty children screaming through their nostril holes

and God's voice is your own voice multiplied by a
thousand and God's voice is that bellerin' steer you
shot down in the desert and God's voice is a whsiperin'
fire sawin' out of that oil drum and can you please pass
the barbecue sauce, *goddamn* that tastes good! You taste
that, soldier?! It tastes just like chicken, like the most
succulent chicken you ever held in your mouth, who
woulda thought that that little sand nigger girl with
the—

(DOTHAN goes mad.)

*(AIKIN enters with a bouquet of purple flowers, gently
pushes the flowers into DOTHAN's face. DOTHAN stops
talking. The flowers gives him pleasure, makes him forget,
brings him to his knees. AIKIN comforts him.)*

(The LOST CHOIR sings an elegiac version of River
Children.*)*

*(During the song, AIKIN picks the remaining purple flowers
out of the earth, turns to a man in the audience.)*

AIKIN: 'Scuse me, sir, you got twenty cent? I just run
outta funds and I gotta get my momma some medicine.
She been laid up wif the trichinoma *(He turns to another
audience member).* Sir, please? Them worms got to her.
She got a lungfrost. She in a bad way *(He turns to a
woman)* Ma'am, you ever seen what the trichinoma
does to a body? Twenty cent cain't be too much to part
wif. *(To another person)* What about you, sir?...
(He exits, as sad and lonesome as he's ever been in his life.)

(The "River Children" Elegy continues.)

*(The WOLF enters with an enormous coiled rope and a
watering can. He waters the dirt mound, then sets down the
rope in the center of the mound, exits.)*

*(PIN enters quickly, lured by the power of the rope. He
approaches it, muscles it onto his shoulder. He then reaches*

down and grabs a fistful of dirt, opens his mouth, closes it, spreads the dirt in his armpits, his chest, his stomach.)

(PIN exits with the rope.)

(The WOLF re-enters, snaps his fingers, ending the River Children *elegy and changing the lights.)*

WOLF: So back to the night of our story—the night in question. Ansel Pinwood becomes Tana's greatest, most heroic advocate and knots that rope to a three-hundred-year-old mossy oak tree, a tree older than three of you, and swims it across the river. You may have felt him slippin' right through your hands, slitherin' between your legs, ticklin' the soles of your feet. Yeah, a river can get tickled, too. Go head and laugh, it's okay.
(He laughs a great crazy laugh.)

(PIN enters with the rope tied around his waist. The WOLF and the LOST CHOIR laugh at him. He is a hysterical, pathetic sight. The WOLF kills the laughter, taunts PIN, torments him over the following:)

WOLF: He endured an awful, turbulent current. Y'all were in a rare mood that night. So many strange things been dumped in that river. Picnic tables. Car parts. Lawn furniture and cigarette machines. I think there might even be an ice cream truck in there somewhere. Mr Softy, drowned like the town drunk… Not to mention the many creatures. The sauger and the muskellunge. The crappie and the walleye and the big horny-faced catfish. The sheephead and the sturgeon. Buffalofish and pike. The many, many snakes. Yeah, they nipped at him. They bit at his flesh and hung on when they could. But he was determined. He might have been the most determined man in the world.

(As the rope rises over the audience, the ensemble chants the following:)

ENSEMBLE: There's a story in the bible about how God turns this donkey into a glass of milk. And the milk gets drunk up by a mountain goat that burps it onto a toad that gets swallowed by Chewbacka before he became a famous actor. I think there might be a Olympic dogsled involved in this arrangement, too. The point is, you can change. You really can. It's right there in the Bible.

(The rope now cuts a diagonal line across the playing space, bowing slightly in the middle.)

*(*DOTHAN *offers his headphones to the* WOLF. *They are attached to nothing but they contain the sound in his head; the sound he's been searching for.)*

DOTHAN: *(To the* WOLF*)* He shredded the trees and broke the ground and finally found the perfect sound.

(The WOLF *listens to the headphones, crosses to the refrigerator, sets the headphones inside, closes the refrigerator door, waits a moment, opens it, and removes the toy drum, crosses to* DOTHAN, *offers the toy drum to him.* DOTHAN *accepts it, places it around his neck, begins to drum a four-four tribal beat. There is an instant deliverance at play, an inevitable spell.)*

(It is now the endless night.)

WOLF: The night is beset by infernal conditions. It's the kind of intolerable, rabid heat that stings the jellies of the eyes and gives rise to the disorders of slowness and stupidity. The Moon is a sickled leopard's tooth pinned to obsidian, its light softly silvering the violent undulations scoring the skin of your unforgiving water. Spiders and worms conspire to spin the lustrous silks of lunacy. The night owl's hoots are quick invisible daggers. Treefrogs bark like hellhounds contorted in attitudes of frenzied madness. The throb of cicadas is so intense it feels like it's coming from inside you.

Just as our young heroine sets out on her journey, three
figures emerge at the edge of the water... Ghostly.
Soul-blighted and mimosa–eyed. Have they risen from
the shoulders of your warm dung-colored banks or are
they the product of more mysterious sources? Have
they materialized from the breath of Hades? Or the
molecular vapors of antediluvian creatures no longer
known to man?

(MONTY, AIKIN *and* DOTHAN *enter the circle, though
hardly recognizable. Their teeth are spired, their eyes wild.)*

*(In the center of the circle, they antique each other's faces
with flour and water. They mark their chests and faces with
blood. Their mouths have grown spired fangs. They have lost
their names. They now are the animal in all of us.)*

WOLF: They take to the mud, making shapes that
are neither human, nor animal, but something more
peculiar. They are forms straddling the thin liminal
faultlines separating man and scorpion, man and
mamba, man and the hackle-backed hyena. Their flesh
thickens and spreads. Their extremities flail about. The
very plasma in their blood is charged with a strange,
larval tonic. Soon the paste on their teeth will be
glazed with syrup not known to you or I. And with a
quickening of this night their quarry—this simple girl
in slow deliberate transit—will no longer be making
her way without duress.

(TANA appears on the rope.)

WOLF: And lo and behold our young heroine appears
on the historic rope that had been threaded so
courageously across the expanse of your water by one
Ansel Pinwood!

*(Beneath the rope DOTHAN, AKIN and MONTY enact
a primitive, ritualistic dance that is by turns, wolf-like,
Pentecostal, magical, their three bodies vectoring across the
space, wiggling like snakes, twisting beneath TANA.)*

WOLF: With only the clothes on her back, Tana Weed makes her way, hand over hand, inch-by-inch, shuttling like some cave-dwelling anthropoid from the time of fire and amphibians, her ankles conjoined with a purpose she has perhaps never known.

(TANA *makes her way across the rope, clinging to it for dear life.*)

WOLF: But the distance she must traverse is considerable and fatigue sets in. The sinews of her arms and legs start to spasm and burn. The flesh of her hands tears away. Her wrists begin to swell with the milk of failure. She bares her teeth at the Night, summoning every angstrom of will that has been assigned to her slight, vernal, unbroken body.
The three figures taunt at her from below, your currents inconsequential to their pursuits as they are now part crocodile, part snapping turtle, part cottonmouth.

(MONTY, AIKIN, *and* DOTHAN *bare their monstrous, spired teeth. They hiss and taunt* TANA *from below the rope, tumbling and vectoring through the mists.*)

(PIN *appears at the other end of the rope, wide-eyed and hopeful.*)

WOLF: And what ho! Ansel Pinwood himself appears at the other end of this umbilical monstrosity, heroic and eager-eyed, gold, valiant warmth filling his throat. He can see that Tana is struggling, that her knuckles are pearling with desperation. He knows full well that she might not make it across. So he goes to her.

(PIN *scuttles across the rope, approaches* TANA, *can't quiet get to her.*)

WOLF: But this act of heroism incites the three creatures hellbent on capturing their prey and, though his initial intentions are indeed valiant and as heroic as one could possibly be, the three others cry out sibilantly.

(MONTY, AIKIN, and DOTHAN cry out, screeching, hissing, hectoring. A distinct warning to PIN to return to them.)

WOLF: Ansel Pinwood reaches out to help Tana, but a blade of moonlight is forced into his eye.

(MONTY blinds PIN with light. The animal sounds of the three hunters reach a frenzied pitch.)

WOLF: And the mesmeric helices of their sounds start to spiral in his mind. There is indefatigable will in his heart, but there is also something rotten; a malignant abscess, small as the eye of a maggot, which may never heal. He can taste the sweets of this night coating his own teeth now. And something falls away inside him. He can feel the best version of himself hurtling backwards through the infinite prism of his soul like a stone hurled from the top of a canyon.

(PIN starts to make sounds like the other three. He fights it but can't help himself. It's as if they're pulling the sounds out of his throat.)

WOLF: Ansel Pinwood, drunk with confusion, must make a choice.

(The creatures taunt PIN, who sobs with frustration. He looks to TANA lovingly, but lowers his hand, then releases the rope, and falls into the water.)

WOLF: And like so many others who've attempted this difficult passage, he is lost to you, Oh Great River. He perishes like a handful of milkweed indifferently grabbed by the wind.

(Members of the LOST CHOIR, who have also transformed into more primitive versions of themselves, pull him through the mists, into darkness.)

WOLF: At that precise moment it's as if a scourge of wasps and locusts has been unleashed. Tana grasps the rind of rope with all her might, but sometimes one's might is limited by circumstance.

(The relentless spell of music ceases for a moment, transforms into something far away and beautiful.)

WOLF: One can hold onto an image in one's head like the flame of a candle. A fallen leaf pressed into wax paper. A wounded swallow peering through one eye, with nothing but its smallness to negotiate mercy. That first surprising snowfall, silvering the world. A doll. A communion cake. The bright periwinkle blue of a forgotten toy...

(TANA loses her grip, falls into the WOLF's arms. He turns her gracefully and lowers her to the earth.)

WOLF: And with a lightness attributed to a child's coat she too is in the river, battling to keep her head above water. She swims her arms and kicks her feet with everything she has but your relentless current takes hold and in less time that it takes to properly clean a fish you've pushed her back to the shore from whence she started. Tana Weed finds herself catching her breath at the base of that old mossy oak. The tree looming above her, its meticulous history contorting through ancient, knobby branches.
The three figures emerge through the skin of your shore like a malignant trinity rising through some unfathomable reverse baptismal. A sense of terrible certainty taints the air. A taste of fresh pewter takes hold. Like a cold bitter spoon thrust between the lips. As this triumvirate progress through the muddy shoals, Tana Weed has nowhere to turn. She can only go in one direction, so she heads back through the trees, fighting clouds of gnats and blood midges.

(TANA starts racing around the perimeter of the circle of chairs. She runs for her life. The three others progress slowly, deliberately around the inner circle, in step, following her with their heads. As she runs three members of the

LOST CHOIR *draw their muddy fingers across her like tree branches. The* WOLF *follows her run with a flashlight.)*

WOLF: She scurries through the very bramble and hollyhock blossoms that marked her secret path to the river. And wouldn't you know it, in what could be a matter of minutes, breaths, and thunderclaps, Tana Weed, sister of Dothan and daughter to all that is dispossessed and wretched in this world, finds herself crossing the threshold of the house she had just fled; that small, colorless tarpaper house she has resided in her entire brief life. The very smell of it is as certain as the sap that bleeds from the arthritic sugar maple in the back yard and the faulty floorboards that release aching dolorous vowels each time she crosses the slender, dusty room where she's slept for the past sixteen years.

Once in the kitchen, Tana heads for the refrigerator, where a simple bag of flour awaits her tired, rope-bitten hands.

*(*TANA *sprints to the refrigerator, opens it, removes the bag of flour, moves to the center of the circle, makes a circle of flour around herself.)*

WOLF: And just as she completes the circle that might provide deliverance from this awful night, three others enter the kitchen, barely recognizable, only vague figurants from the life she was fleeing, jackal-eyed and wanton, as far from the thoughts of Man as a falcon from the molten stalactite's of Hell.

(The figures who were once MONTY, AIKIN *and* DOTHAN *close in on* TANA, *remaining outside the perimeter of flour.)*

*(*TANA *can see, smell, taste, feel, and hear everything. For a moment we hear only her labored respirations and nothing else.)*

(Out of the darkness DEBO *materializes.)*

MAN: And at that very moment a text message transmits onto the face of Tana Weed's phone: "Tana, I'm at the bus depot. Got here early just in case... We fixed up the guest room today. I hope you like it. I just washed the car... "

(The WOLF snaps his fingers and the lights come up, illuminating the audience.)

WOLF: *(To the audience)* So this is where thing's get real interesting. Y'all are gonna have an opportunity to stop all this.

The rules are simple. All that's gotta happen is one of you has to stand up, depart from the comfort of your carefully selected chair, enter that circle of flour there, and take that girl by the hand and lead her out of here...

(The WOLF allows the audience to consider his proposition.)

WOLF: *(To the audience)* You can do it, you really can. Just go on up there and show her the way. Walk her right through those doors there... No? ...What about you, sir? ...Ma'am?

(TANA soundlessly pleads with the final solicited member of the audience.)

(If a member of the audience rises from their seat, crosses into the circle of flour, takes TANA's hand, and leads her out of the theatre, then the play ends and an incredible celebration ensues involving dance, music, confetti, drinks, and celebratory cake all around. If the audience doesn't respond, then this happens:)

WOLF: Well, y'all are the river.

(The WOLF snaps, triggering an unbearable heartbeat. Lights fade to black as the three figures close in on TANA.)

(Lights up to reveal a tableau of TANA being torn asunder. It is a savage, brutal death. They pull her limbs off and devour her like wolves.)

(Somewhere in the theater, PIN *appears as a ghost.)*

(After the final blackout, lights come up to reveal her torn dress, panties, jean shorts, and shoes in the center of the circle of flour.)

END OF PLAY